IF I WERE A...

CANINE

WRITTEN BY
CHARIS MATHER

WINDMILL
BOOKS™

Published in 2025 by Windmill Books,
an Imprint of Rosen Publishing
2544 Clinton St.
Buffalo, NY 14224

Written by:
Charis Mather

Edited by:
E.C. Andrews

Designed by:
Ker Ker Lee

Cataloging-in-Publication Data
Names: Mather, Charis, 1999-.
Title: Canine / Charis Mather.
Description: Buffalo, NY : Windmill Books, 2025. | Series: If I were a… | Includes glossary and index.
Identifiers: ISBN 9781538398043 (pbk.) | ISBN 9781538398050 (library bound) | ISBN 9781538398067 (ebook)
Subjects: LCSH: Dogs--Juvenile literature. | Canidae--Juvenile literature. | Wild dogs--Juvenile literature. | Wolves--Juvenile literature.
Classification: LCC SF426.5 M376 2025 | DDC 599.77--dc23

Printed in the United States of America

CPSIA Compliance Information: Batch #CW25WM
For Further Information contact Rosen Publishing at 1-800-237-9932

Find us on

Photo Credits – Images are courtesy of Shutterstock.com. With thanks to Getty Images, Thinkstock Photo and iStockphoto.

Characters – yusufdemirci. Recurring images – Sachiko Nakai. Cover – Andrew Molinaro, Vlada Cech, Miroslav Hlavko, Prostock-studio. 2–3 – Ondrej Prosicky. 4–5 – Paleokastritsa. 6–7 – cynoclub, Haletska Olha, AnetaZabranska, Glikiri, New Africa. 8–9 – Allison Coffin, Jim Cumming. 10–11 – Michal Ninger, Sophia Granchinho. 12–13 – JEcoPrint, Eric Isselee, Etienne Outram, AgnesSz. 14–15 – Yongyut Kumsri, Jan-Hendrik van Rooyen. 16–17 – Stanislav Duben, Vladimir Chernyanskiy. 18–19 – stefbennett, Josef_Svoboda. 20–21 – Teguh Mujionow, Ondrej Prosicky, Vaclav Sebek.

CONTENTS

Words that look like <u>this</u> can be found in the glossary on page 24.

COOL CANINES

It must be cool to be a canine.

A CANINE IS AN ANIMAL FROM THE DOG FAMILY.

Canines can be very friendly or very fierce. Even though canines have lots in common, each different kind has its own characteristics that make it stand out.

If you were a canine, what would you be? Would you be big or small? Would you be part of a pack or go solo? There are so many kinds of canines to choose from!

DOMESTIC DOG

<u>Domestic</u> dogs are among the friendliest animals in the world. Lots of domestic dogs live with humans and have very close <u>relationships</u> with them. Many dogs are very clever and playful.

There are hundreds of different domestic dog breeds.

DOGS THAT HAVE PARENTS OF DIFFERENT BREEDS ARE CALLED CROSSBREEDS.

WOLF

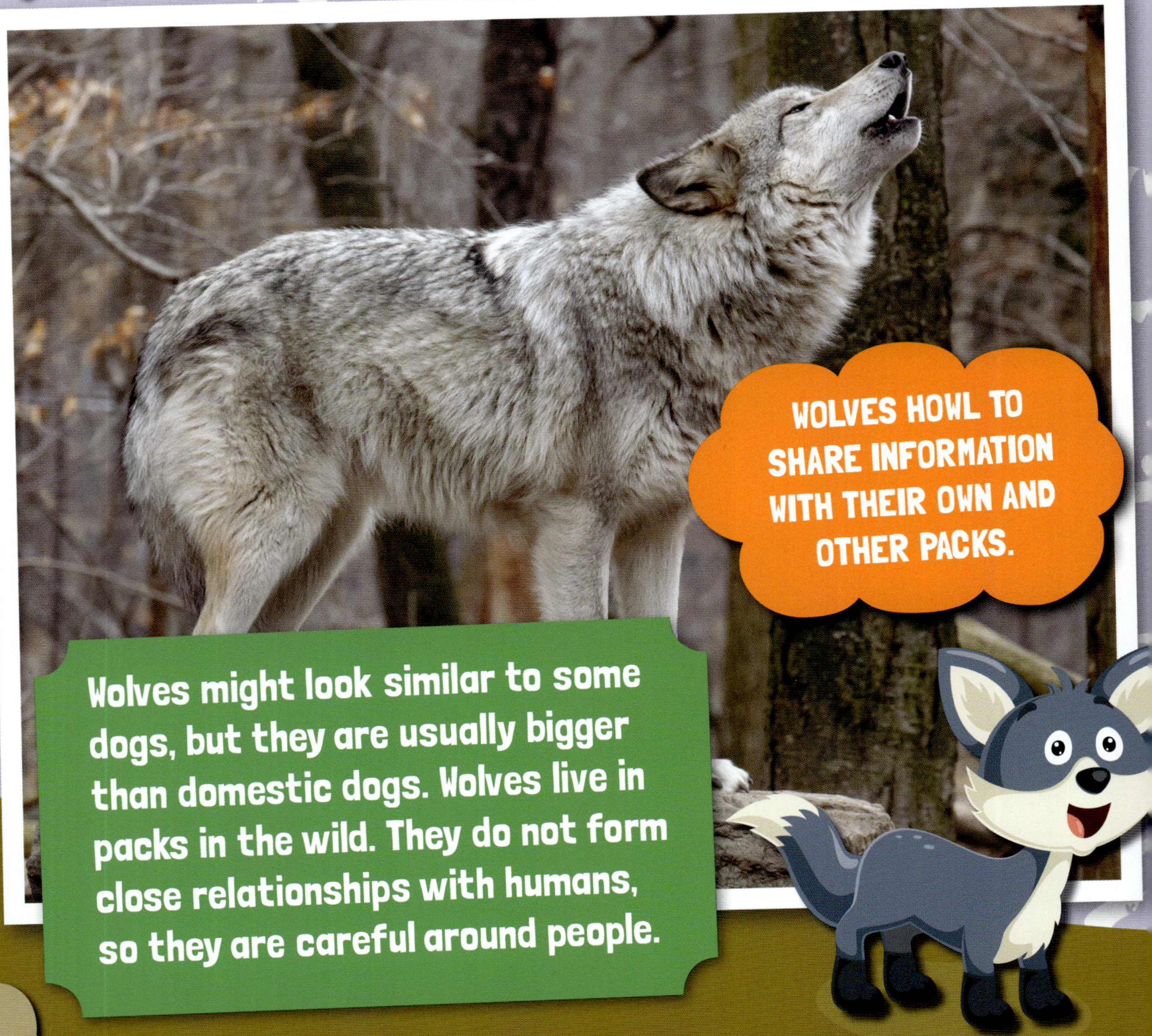

WOLVES HOWL TO SHARE INFORMATION WITH THEIR OWN AND OTHER PACKS.

Wolves might look similar to some dogs, but they are usually bigger than domestic dogs. Wolves live in packs in the wild. They do not form close relationships with humans, so they are careful around people.

Wolf packs work together to look after their wolf pups. They teach the young wolves how to live in the wild. Packs also take care of old and injured wolves.

I would be a wolf. They care about their pack!

FOX

Foxes are small canines with bushy tails. There are many different kinds.

RED FOX

Red foxes can mostly be found in forests. Their coats are a red-orange color with a white tip.

ARCTIC FOX

Arctic foxes live in the Arctic, where it is often very cold. Their thick white fur helps them blend in with the snow. This helps them hide from other animals.

BAT-EARED FOX

Bat-eared foxes have huge ears that help them keep cool in their warm, dry <u>habitats</u>.

Bat-eared foxes get their name from their big, bat-like ears!

Most foxes hunt small animals, such as mice, rabbits, and birds. However, bat-eared foxes mainly eat insects.

Most foxes prefer to live on their own or in very small groups. However, bat-eared foxes do not mind sharing the same area with each other.

JACKAL

I would be a jackal because jackals look out for their families.

Jackals are very vocal. This means that they make lots of different noises, such as growls, yaps, hoots, and howls. They pay close attention to any warning sounds or calls for help from their family.

Lots of animals have different **mates** throughout their lives. However, once a jackal has found a mate, they stay with that mate for the rest of their lives.

JACKALS USUALLY WORK IN PAIRS TO HUNT AND PROTECT THEIR HOMES.

RACCOON DOG

I would be a raccoon dog so that I could climb trees!

Raccoon dogs look very similar to raccoons, but they are completely different animals. It is unusual for canines to climb trees. However, raccoon dogs have curved claws that make them great climbers.

It is also unusual for canines to hibernate, but raccoon dogs do this too. This means that they rest through the coldest parts of the year to save their energy for the warmer days.

BUSH DOG

Bush dogs are short little canines, but that does not mean that they are cute and cuddly. With their pack, bush dogs can hunt down prey that are much bigger than they are.

BUSH DOGS ARE SOMETIMES CALLED VINEGAR DOGS BECAUSE THEY SMELL LIKE VINEGAR!

Bush dogs do not just hunt on land. Their bodies are perfect for swimming. They sometimes chase their prey into water, where it is harder for their prey to escape.

AFRICAN WILD DOG

African wild dogs stand out because of their coats. They have patches of black, brown, yellow, and white fur. They are sometimes called painted dogs because of this. They have big ears and long legs.

When they work together, African wild dogs are some of the world's best hunters. Their excellent teamwork helps them catch most of the prey they go after, so they hardly ever miss a meal.

You will not often see African wild dogs without their pack.

WHAT WOULD YOU BE?

What would you be?

GLOSSARY

breeds groups of animals in the same species that have certain traits in common

characteristics features of a living thing that help to identify it

domestic not wild; often tamed and kept by humans

energy the power that makes living things able to move and live

family a group of animals that have certain features in common

habitats the natural homes in which animals, plants, and other living things live

mates partners that animals choose to produce young with

pack a group of animals who live and hunt with each other

prey animals that are hunted by other animals for food

relationships meaningful connections between two or more people or animals

INDEX